When I Was 40

When I Was 40

Overcame Some Challenges,

Still Learning and Growing

Charlene Stevens Jenkins

XULON PRESS

Xulon Press
2301 Lucien Way #415
Maitland, FL 32751
407.339.4217
www.xulonpress.com

© 2020 by Charlene Stevens Jenkins

All rights reserved solely by the author. The author guarantees all contents are original and do not infringe upon the legal rights of any other person or work. No part of this book may be reproduced in any form without the permission of the author. The views expressed in this book are not necessarily those of the publisher.

Unless otherwise indicated, Scripture quotations taken from the King James Version (KJV) – *public domain*.

Scripture quotations taken from the New King James Version (NKJV). Copyright © 1982 by Thomas Nelson, Inc. Used by permission. All rights reserved.

Scripture quotations taken from the Holy Bible, New International Version (NIV). Copyright © 1973, 1978, 1984, 2011 by Biblica, Inc.™. Used by permission. All rights reserved.

Printed in the United States of America.

Paperback ISBN-13: 978-1-6305-0957-6

Ebook ISBN-13: 978-1-6305-0958-3

Dedication and Acknowledgments

This book is dedicated to the memory of my deceased husband, Benjamin Jenkins, because he encouraged and supported my decision to write it one day.

I also dedicate this to my children: Paul Williams, Jr.; Jessica Jenkins; and Camilla Johnson (Aaron); my parents, Joseph Charles Stevens, Sr. and Jean Stevens; my siblings: Joseph Charles Stevens, Jr.; Denesia Roberts (Christopher); and Kimberly Porter; my second parents, Donald and Patricia O'Nery; all of my nieces, nephews, aunts, uncles, cousins, pastors, and spiritual leaders, prayer partners, mentors, mentees, supporters, loved ones, and friends.

To my late grandparents: Paul Stevens, Sr. and Janie Stevens; Isaiah (MC) Johnson and Hattie Johnson.

This book is also dedicated to every person who has faced or is currently facing challenges and decisions to stand firm on your faith in God. Don't give up.

God, thank You for every blessing I received and for every difficulty I've had to endure. Psalm 34:1 encourages me to bless Your name at all times. Over the years, I have discovered that You do not waste any of my pain. You can use the pain that I brought upon myself and the pain inflicted upon me by others. Thank You for inspiring me to write and may this book be a source of encouragement, inspiration, and motivation to others.

Table of Contents

Dedication and Acknowledgments v
Introduction ix

Chapter 1–Closing a Chapter.........................1
Chapter 2–Still Called, Still Favored................ 13
Chapter 3–Me? Yes, You........................... 25
Chapter 4–A New Home **and** a New Job? 41
Chapter 5–Steps Ordered 55
Chapter 6–Visible Difference 67

Epilogue 83
More Reflections 91
Final Word of Encouragement from Charlene 95
About the Author.................................. 97

Introduction

I was born in Riceboro, Georgia, on the way to the Hinesville Hospital, which is now known as Liberty Regional Medical Center. Back then, it was located on Highway 84, the present site of the Liberty County Department of Family and Children Services. Mama told me that I was born in my maternal grandmother's car, so I must have been in a hurry to get here. Because I am only five feet tall, I always walk as if I am in a hurry now. My parents are J.C. Stevens, Sr. and Jean Stevens. I was blessed to grow up knowing three of my four grandparents, Paul Stevens, Sr., Hattie Johnson, and Isaiah (MC) Johnson. I am the oldest of four. I have a brother and two sisters: Joseph Stevens, Jr., Denesia Roberts (Christopher), and Kimberly Porter. I also have some precious nieces and nephews.

Before my parents built their current home, we lived right off Highway 17, just a couple of miles up the road from Interstate 95. I have been in church for as long as I can remember and grew up attending what is now the Kingdom Church of Christ, Holiness Unto the Lord. Because I lived in Liberty County until marriage, I went to school in Hinesville from the first to twelfth grades. Kindergarten was not mandatory for me. I graduated from Bradwell Institute in 1987 and attended my freshman year at Savannah State College.

I took a break from school and got married to Paul Williams in 1988. Our only son was born in 1998. In January of 2001, I started ministers' training and finally returned to Savannah State University at the age of thirty-one. In June, I was licensed as a gospel minister and ordained in December of 2002. I earned a Bachelor of Social Work degree in 2006 and a Master of Social Work degree in 2007.

The main focal point of this book is the span of time when I was about to turn forty until around my forty-first birthday, so I will fast forward to June of 2009. Some authors have called this time in life...*halftime.* At halftime in a football game, the team reviews the first half of the game, then makes changes in strategy and attitude to play better and win in the second half. Bob Buford in his book, *Halftime,* writes:

> "As you take stock, ask yourself these similar questions: What is my passion? How am I wired? Where do I belong? What do I believe? What will I do about what I believe? Or, as Peter Drucker advised people who were looking for their life's task: What are my values, my aspirations, my directions, and what do I have to do, to learn, to change, in order to make myself

capable of living up to my demands on myself and my expectations of life?"

-Bob P. Buford, *Halftime: Changing Your Game Plan from Success to Significance*[1]

As I think back, so many historic events took place that year. One was that the presidency of Barack Obama began at **noon EST on January 20, 2009, when he** was inaugurated as the 44th President of the United States. He served until January 20, 2017. That was such a memorable event! I can recall sitting in front of the TV watching the inauguration of America's very first African American president! I could hardly believe my eyes. I sat there in awe and I could not stop thanking God for letting me live to see that day.

By the end of 2009, I realized I had experienced quite a few memorable events of my own, which prompted the title of this book. I have taken pride in my accomplishments. I have had time to think about some decisions I made and challenges I faced.

I was thinking about something recently. Many people in their forties and fifties find themselves in a midlife crisis. Maybe something has happened, or something was done that caused a disruption in the home—a lost job, a lost business, bankruptcy, a failed marriage, a loved one's death, an empty nest, unfulfilled goals and dreams, and the list goes on.

---

[1] https://www.goodreads.com/work/quotes/14735843-halftime-changing-your-game-plan-from-success-to-significance

My disruption was a failed marriage. Although I initiated the divorce, the process was still devastating. I could have allowed that low period to define the rest of my life. All sorts of things played over in my mind, especially things like, "I'm getting old and I never imagined I'd be going through this!"

By the way, some people think that forty is old. *I* used to think forty was old until I turned forty. When I finally started writing this book, I was making plans for how I would celebrate my fiftieth birthday!

In November 2018, Former First Lady, Michelle Obama released her memoir, "Becoming." My baby sister, Kimberly, and her children gave me the book for Christmas. NBC News reported earlier in 2019 that it was set to become the best-selling memoir in history. It was easy to do a Google search and discover that "Becoming" had sold more copies than any other book published in the United States in 2018 and broke the record in just fifteen days! Congratulations, Mrs. Obama!

Mrs. Obama's tour brought her to Atlanta on May 11, 2019. I was so grateful that my son blessed me with a very early Mother's Day and birthday gift the week after Christmas. My best friend, prayer partner, Women's Conference roommate, and travel buddy, Philisa LeGrier, and I had our tickets before January 1! It would be an understatement to say we had an amazing time. Atlanta was tour #33, with Michelle Obama and Gayle King. It is not surprising that it sold out at every location. Mrs. Obama is such a dynamic speaker! I cannot recap everything she shared with us; however, I will mention Mrs. Obama said, "People, welcome your hardships. Those trials and tribulations prepare you for the future." I really enjoyed reading her book, and I certainly agree with that statement.

I turned fifty in June of 2019. I have learned so much about myself and I have grown tremendously. I sincerely hope that after you read this book, you will...

- Be encouraged to reflect on your life with all the insights you gained about your strengths and challenges.
- Find yourself growing instead of remaining stagnant, as I once was.
- Discover how God is working behind the scenes strengthening you to overcome present obstacles and giving you hope for the future.
- Seek out inspirational role models for your life to motivate you to reach higher levels and achieve greater goals.
- Learn how to love yourself and others with the love God has deposited in your life.

Thank you for holding my book in your hands right now. Maybe you purchased it or it was gifted to you; I am grateful. I sincerely pray it is a blessing to you and to everyone you share it with.

Chapter 1
Closing a Chapter

It is very possible that you have never seen a book begin with the words, "Closing a Chapter." Neither have I, but I chose this title because I was in transition around the age of forty. My marriage to Paul Williams, Sr. was slowly coming to an end. By the way, I had mastered smiling and pretending I was okay around my relatives and church family. In December 2007, I told my parents that we would be separated for a while (about 8 months in 2008) and they were shocked because I had been keeping our problems to myself. During the separation, Paul Jr. and I lived in a duplex, a local hotel, and with my "SisterFriend" Daisy Jones and husband Nathan. Paul Sr. and I reconciled and our son and I moved back home at the beginning of January 2009.

Near the end of that month, Paul Sr. and I had a heated "discussion." Words were spoken that cannot be retracted and events transpired that cannot be undone. No, we did not need law enforcement or medical attention. Thankfully, Paul Jr. was sleeping and did not witness any of it. Lack of proper communication was just a fraction of our deeper, unresolved relationship issues. I do not remember much about the next few months. They were filled with tears as I drove home from work. Tears came as I sat with my Bible not knowing what to read or how to pray.

There were a few happy memories around that time, as well. On my fortieth birthday on June 19, ten of us had dinner at Pelican Point in Crescent, Georgia. It was known for its outstanding seafood buffet. I enjoyed the food and fellowship. Then, just three days later, my baby sister and her husband had their first child, Eli Porter, Jr.

I filed for divorce in July of that year and it was final in September. After our divorce, I told Paul the same thing I said to God, "I'm sorry for anything I did or anything I failed to do that caused our relationship to fall apart." I am still at peace with my decision to leave him (not my son). With those words, I was able to close that chapter in my life so that I could move forward. There is life after divorce. It is possible to thrive and not just survive after the ending of a marriage.

Surrender to the Paintbrush

As I am reflecting on all of this, I must share some excerpts from a message by our Pastor's wife, First Lady Christi Cowart. She spoke this during the Women's Conference at Live Oak Church, Hinesville, Georgia on Friday, November 2, 2018. Her subject was, "I May Be Unfinished, But I'm Not Undone." The main scripture was

Philippians 1:6, "Being confident of this very thing, that He who has begun a good work in you will complete it until the day of Jesus Christ" (NKJV). First Lady said, "I'm always working on a better me." I just love the transparency of our Pastors.

She had some canvases on stage which showed finished paintings. On the screen, we could see the pictures of the paintings from start to finish. First Lady encouraged us to, "Surrender to the paintbrush. What you go through produces character. Stop letting other folks take their paintbrush and paint on your canvas. Let God work. Nobody quits when they mess up. Stop where you are, fix your issue, and move forward. Enjoy every stroke. It's not your speed but your endurance that gets you to the end. Your mistakes don't catch God by surprise. 'They that wait upon the Lord shall renew their strength' (Isaiah 40:31). Don't trade the process for a quick fix. The process prepares you for the promise. Faith is confidence in the character of God."

Other scriptures she used were Hebrews 12:2 and Jeremiah 29:11. She ended with, "We're all unfinished." I could really relate when she said that my mistakes did not catch God by surprise and when I surrender to God, what I go through continues to produce character in me!

The past doesn't determine the future unless we let it.

While I cannot change what happened when my first marriage ended, I can make sure that my actions and my response to my ex-husband still reflect the love of God. Even while writing this book, he texted me an apology! I looked down at my cell phone, and there it was on Saturday, February 9, 2019. At that moment, Philisa and I were on our way to check out after we had picked up a few things at the local Hobby Lobby.

In short, he said, "I apologize and ask for your forgiveness of any and everything that I have ever done to offend or hurt you. I also take responsibility for allowing the devil to destroy our family many years ago."

Repentance involves admitting we did something wrong...taking responsibility, quitting it...that is to say we stop doing what's wrong and just do the right thing, and finally, forgetting it...we move on by forgetting the hurt and releasing forgiveness and love and taking hold of God's plans for us which give us a hope and a future.

I was amazed and speechless. I thanked God that almost ten years after the divorce I received an apology! Later, I responded and told him that I accepted. Before going to bed that night, I felt the need to send these words, "I forgive you." He replied, "Thanks and God bless you."

Years ago, he said that he had apologized, but I did not remember it. This time, it was unforgettable. While writing this book, he remarried, and I congratulated him. I am happy for him and his new wife and family.

The remainder of this book is about how God helped me in so many ways right after the divorce. I was struggling financially, as many people do. I want you to know that God can open doors for you the same way He did for me.

Have you ever literally tried to open two doors at the exact same time? It takes much skill, much concentration, and the doors need to be positioned in such a way that both hands can be utilized simultaneously. Well, I don't go around trying to open more than one door at a time, because I cannot physically enter or exit more than one at a time.

I asked that question because I came to the conclusion: Sometimes God cannot open the new door, until we close the previous door.

• 🖋 •

Also, sometimes God can't take us into the next chapter until we bring closure to some current issues. I am not aware of your situation. You may need to ask yourself, "Am I going to continue on this road or am I going to ask God to show me a detour?" By the way, God can still use our detours, if our goal is to please Him and bring Him glory. Keep reading if you want to find out how God used my detour and some doors He opened for me just six months after the divorce.

Seek Help and Guidance

As I think back to that time, I clearly recall that after I moved out on August 1, 2009, I no longer needed medication for depression and anxiety. I am about to share something that I am not proud of, because we didn't have to end up there. We were both ordained leaders in our church. We did not seek help and guidance early enough because of our pride and shame. We eventually went to our leaders, Pastor M.L. and First Lady Shrye Jackson, for counseling. We also met with two licensed counselors or therapists. Those sessions would have been much more helpful if we had gone sooner.

I must add that when we stopped praying together, our marital problems compounded. I became accustomed to wearing a mask and pretending that everything was okay. Do not let that happen to you. Put your pride aside and ask for help early. Start with someone you trust, with your leadership, and you may need to also seek professional counseling. Now, I would highly suggest having a couple to mentor you. Good, godly mentors could have helped us if we had only drawn from the expertise of the many couples around us. Hindsight is 20/20.

I have come to really understand from personal experience that the family that prays together stays together.

· 𝝋 ·

I have learned that it is vital to pray with my spouse even if I do not feel like doing so. When we are sick, we do not always feel like eating. So why do we make ourselves do it? We force ourselves to take in the necessary nutrition so that we can get back on the road to recovery much quicker. Imagine what will happen in our families if we would persevere and continue to pray together even when we are not that interested in being close to our loved ones. The long-term benefits far outweigh any temporary discomfort.

After we divorced, I repented, God forgave me, and I had a peace about my decision. I was determined not to repeat the same mistakes that led to our conflicts and sometimes days or weeks of hardly speaking to one another. I have finally learned that caring for my family is much more important than operating in the ministry. In fact, I know now that my family is my first ministry. We are the Body of Christ. If the families and homes are out of alignment, then the churches and ministries will be out of alignment.

At the time, I was wearing a mask and was blinded. Now, I clearly see that a chaotic and dysfunctional home will not mysteriously create a growing and healthy ministry for two reasons.

First, *charity begins at home.* I used to think that was in the Bible until I tried to find it and discovered it is not there. My interpretation of that is the love of Jesus must begin where I live, then spread outward to where I work, and then to where I worship.

The people we live with and the people we work with must see Jesus in us.

We spend more time with them than we do the people at church. For that reason, if family members and coworkers cannot see the fruit of the Spirit in operation in our lives, but the people at church can, then I believe we could be putting on a show or we are not letting our lights shine at all times.

Second, *the foundation of a spiritually healthy church is a spiritually healthy home or family unit.* If I am stagnant at home, it is very likely that I will be stagnant at church or as I said before, I will be pretending at church. It is best to live knowing that God can see us 24/7, and if we remind ourselves of that, it will greatly impact how we live, the choices we make, and what we do both in public and in private.

One day, I was tired of the pretense and stagnation. I confess I had trouble praying for the marriage because I no longer wanted to be there. After the divorce, I told God that if it was ever His will for me to get married again, I needed Him to work on me. I did not want to take any bad habits or negative mindsets into a new relationship. God answered that prayer. I married Ben in 2013. Every day, we tried our best to laugh, pray, and talk, and we did this until he passed away in 2014. I am so grateful for God's forgiveness, for new opportunities, and that even in the middle of disappointments, I still have God's favor!

Chapter 1
Closing a Chapter Reflections

What have you discovered that may need to be challenged, changed, or confronted in your own life?

_____

_____

How are you going to deal with this?

_____

_____

What are you going to do differently?

_____

_____

When I Was 40

Where will you start?

_____

_____

With whom will you share your concerns?

_____

_____

When will you do that?

_____

_____

Take a few minutes to look up and reflect on the scriptures given in this chapter. Record what the Holy Spirit reveals to you from these scriptures as they relate to your life situation.

Isaiah 40:31 tells me if I

_____

_____

Hebrews 12:2 tells me I need to

_____

_____

Closing A Chapter Reflections

Jeremiah 29:11 assures me

_____

_____

Philippians 1:6 promises me

_____

_____

Important Points and Notes from this Chapter

_____

_____

_____

_____

_____

_____

_____

_____

_____

_____

Pray: *God, I am so grateful for Your forgiveness, for new opportunities, and that even in the middle of disappointments, I still have Your favor.*

Chapter 2
Still Called, Still Favored

Yes, it is possible to live a blessed, happy, and fulfilled life after a divorce. By no means am I recommending that you divorce your spouse! I said that because I have learned that the ending of a relationship with a *person* does not mean that my relationship with God has ended. In fact, it is during that difficult time when I found myself more focused on God. I learned that...

Failing in marriage, or any failure, never means that God gives up on us or will no longer use us. God never gives up on us even when we give up on Him!

Called and Favored

While growing up in church over the years, I often heard the words *called* and *favored*, and I want to take a few moments to define them.

According to the *Handbook of Bible Application*, *call* means "assignment, ministry, vocation." Paraphrasing and adapting what this handbook says...

God's Purpose: *What Does God Call People to Do?*

Bible Reading: Jeremiah 1:1-10 Key Bible Verse: "Before I formed you in the womb I knew you, before you were born I set you apart; I appointed you as a prophet to the nations" (Jeremiah 1:5 NIV).

God calls people to serve Him. Jeremiah was "appointed" by God "as a prophet to the nations." God has a purpose for each Christian, but some people are appointed by God for specific kinds of work.

God calls people to represent Him in the world. Jesus called His twelve disciples. He didn't draft them, force them, or ask them to volunteer; He chose them to serve Him in a special way. Christ calls us today. He doesn't twist our arms and make us do something we don't want to do. We can choose to join Him or remain behind.

According to Baker's Evangelical Dictionary of Biblical Theology, *finding favor* means gaining approval, acceptance, or special benefits or blessings. There is also a close association between favor, grace, and mercy, which are sometimes used to translate the same Hebrew and Greek words (such as *hen [ej]* and *charis [cavri]*). The favor that human beings receive from God depends on His good pleasure and is often extended in response to prayer or righteous living. Gabriel told Mary in Luke 1:30 that she had "found favor with God."[2]

So, even while experiencing the discord that eventually led to a divorce, I had to remind myself that I was still called to do a specific work for God and that I still had His favor upon my life to accomplish that work.

On June 30, 2009, the lesson from "Our Daily Bread" was titled "Macauley," and the scripture was Isaiah 6:1-8.

Verse 8 says, "Also I heard the voice of the Lord saying, Whom shall I send, and who will go for Us? Then said I, Here am I; send me" (NKJV).

When I read that, I thought about Romans 11:29 which says, "For the gifts and calling of God are without repentance" (KJV).

I was going through some things at the time and I had to remind myself that I was still called by God and a minister of the Gospel. I told myself that I was still His child. I prayed that He would continue to use me and that from now on I wanted Him to have His way in my life.

On Wednesday, July 1, 2009, I overslept and had to pray as I drove to work. During that day, Paul Sr. and I met with the legal aid and turned in our paperwork to begin the divorce process. She planned to email the drafts the next day. If there were no changes, we would consent and sign the

---

[2] https://www.biblestudytools.com/dictionaries/bakers-evangelical-dictionary/favor.html

copy the following Monday or Tuesday. After that, it would be filed and would go before the judge in about 31 days.

Later that night, I attended what is now the Kingdom Church of Christ, Darien, Georgia. My first Pastor, Bishop Eddie Lee Stevens, Sr. (who I called Uncle Bishop), prayed for God to give us power, encouragement, and warning from His Word. The speaker was my first cousin, who is now Pastor Robert Bernard Pope (Evangelistic Pentecostal Church, Darien).

He opened his message with, "Learn all you can about what God has called you to do. Whatever you do for God, do it wholeheartedly." The scripture was Ephesians 1:1-23. The subject of his message was, "Where Is This Christ? In Me!" He continued with, "If we were predestined, that means God knew ahead of time that each of us would be here. As we seek Him, He guides and directs us."

Because of the events from earlier in the day, I was somewhat distracted. I usually take a lot of notes, but I did not do much writing this night, but here is one more relevant point he shared.

"When you're going through trials, having problems in your home, or on your job, if Christ is in you, nothing can stop you."

After the message, the speaker invited us to come forward for prayer. I decided to get in line. When I stood before him, he said, "God said that no matter what has happened and no matter what decisions have been made, My favor is upon you." He anointed my head and prayed for me. I was so grateful, and I praised God for not leaving me. I needed to hear those words! I was up there feeling like less than a Christian and less than a minister because of the decision to end our marriage.

After the service, we hugged and talked. I was able to let him know of the events that had transpired just hours earlier. What he said was something like this:

Regardless of where you turn, You cannot escape God's will for you.

Yes, I was in the middle of a divorce, but I was still called, and there was still work for me to do.

Now that I am fifty and I have had the opportunity to reflect on all of that, I am blessed and encouraged. God never left me! I might have made mistakes along the way, but He still favors me, and I am eternally grateful!

Maybe you have felt the same way that I did. I have learned that because I repented, I am forgiven. It is the enemy who tries to make me feel condemned. The word says, "There is therefore now no condemnation to those who are in Christ Jesus" (Romans 8:1 NKJV).

I found encouragement in reading the story of David and Bathsheba and how God sent the prophet Nathan to guide him. David repented and God continued to use him. In fact, God refers to David as a man after His own heart in spite of his poor decisions (see 2 Samuel chapters 11-12).

David was a man after God's heart, not because he was perfect, but because he repented.

• 𝜙 •

My goal is to live a life of repentance. Currently in my life, I am intentionally avoiding plans that could lead to sin, but whenever I make a mistake, I try to repent quickly. I have learned to apologize quickly if I have a disagreement with someone. I do not have to say the last word anymore. I have matured tremendously as I am learning how to be a woman after God's heart.

Chapter 2
Still Called, Still Favored
Reflections

Have you ever felt like you could not continue to serve in an area of ministry because of a past mistake or because of sin?

_____

_____

Have you repented?

_____

_____

Do you believe that God has forgiven you?

_____

_____

When I Was 40

Do you want to be restored?

_____

_____

Do you desire to continue serving?

_____

_____

What will you do differently?

_____

_____

Whom will you discuss your concerns with?

_____

_____

When?

_____

_____

Take a few minutes to look up and reflect on the scriptures given in this chapter. Record what the Holy Spirit reveals to you from these scriptures as they relate to your life situation.

Still Called, Still Favored Reflections

Read Jeremiah 1:1-10. Jeremiah 1:5 tells me I am

_____

_____

In Luke 1:30, what did the angel Gabriel tell Mary?

_____

_____

In Isaiah 6:8, what question did God ask?

_____

_____

How will you answer this question?

_____

_____

What does Romans 11:29 say about the gifts and calling of God?

_____

_____

What does that mean to you?

_____

_____

What does Ephesians 1:11 say about God's will for you?

_____

_____

What is the promise for you in Romans 8:1?

_____

_____

What did you discern from the story of David in 2 Samuel chapters 11-12?

_____

_____

Important Points and Notes from this Chapter

_____

_____

_____

_____

_____

_____

_____

_____

_____

Pray: *Father God, please help me to repent quickly when I make a mistake, apologize quickly when I have a disagreement with someone, and show me how to reflect Your heart to those in my area of influence at home, work, and in my church. Please confirm the call You have on my life and continue to use me to serve in Your kingdom work. I want You to have Your way in my life.*

Chapter 3
Me? Yes, You

My marriage to Paul Sr. began on December 17, 1988, and our divorce was final on September 2, 2009. For most of 2009, I intentionally avoided attending the Holy Communion service, which was on the first Wednesday night of each month. I *chose* not to go because of my relationship at home. I did not want to face the "damnation" mentioned in I Corinthians 11:29 that was read at each communion service. I had already planned to start attending again in January of 2010.

The church secretary, Sister Sarah Stevens, called me on Monday, November 30, 2009 (Kimberly's birthday). I was a social worker for DaVita Dialysis Clinics, and on this day, I was scheduled to drive to Metter, Georgia. I was glad that I was not out on the floor with patients and I was available to talk. Sister Sarah let me know that Pastor (now Bishop) M.L. Jackson told her that I would be the speaker for the communion service on Wednesday night.

I was very shocked, especially since I had not attended a communion service at all that year. I even asked if I could wait until January because I felt that I was the *last* person who needed to be speaking to the congregation right now. I wanted to make sure that she was calling the right person, and I wanted to make sure that she told Pastor that I had not been attending (as if he was not already aware). Maybe he would change his mind about having me speak. She put me on hold, talked to Pastor, and when she returned, told me that God told him I was to be the speaker for Wednesday, December 2.

"Yes, ma'am," I said, as the call ended.

Immediately, I told God, "I need You to give me a word."

I told a few intercessors and they were praying with me. Elder Dori (now Pastor Griffin, End Time Harvest Ministries in Midway, Georgia) and Cousin Bernard. Dori gave me Jeremiah 1:8 and said, "Don't be afraid of their faces." Cousin Bernard also encouraged me and said, "You're going back to communion because God missed you at the dinner table. Atonement = at-one-ment. Communion is a sacred act but live at all times holy before God."

Later, I found myself reading I Corinthians 11:29, which states, "Whoever eateth and drinketh unworthily, eateth and drinketh damnation to himself" (KJV). I admitted that I had allowed my disappointments, frustrations, and issues to keep me away and cause me to avoid participating in the communion service. I repented and began preparing myself to go back and preparing myself to speak.

When I spent time in the Word later, I was drawn to Jeremiah 18:1-6 and the title God gave me was, "Broken, Made Over, Made Whole."

> *The word which came to Jeremiah from the Lord, saying, Arise, and go down to the potter's house, and there I will cause thee to hear my words. Then I went down to the potter's house, and behold, he wrought a work on the wheels. And the vessel that he made of clay was marred in the hand of the potter: so he made it again another vessel, as seemed good to the potter to make it. Then the word of the Lord came to me, saying, O house of Israel, cannot I do with you as this potter? Saith the Lord. Behold, as the clay is in the potter's hand, so are ye in mine hand, O house of Israel.* (KJV)

On Tuesday morning, December 1, I was studying from the "Star Book for Ministers" about The Lord's Supper.[3] A few minutes later, I received a call from Dori with a word, "Read Romans 8:28-31. Don't worry about the people who know about the past, who know about the divorce. If God is for you, who can be against you?"

This particular day, I had driven to and from DaVita Dialysis Clinic in Savannah, where I was covering for

---

[3] https://books.google.com/books/about/The_Star_Book_for_Ministers.html?id=5jlNCgAAQBAJ (p.125)

another social worker. I was so tired that I had to drag myself into the shower and I had to lean on the sink to brush my teeth. I could hardly keep my eyes open. I told God, "I'm trusting You to give me the Word for tomorrow night." I went to sleep. I was too tired to eat dinner and woke up hungry around 11:30 p.m. I had a snack and since I had gotten about three hours of sleep, I was ready to get into the Word.

I prayed for wisdom. I continued to study and prepare. Then at 4 a.m., I prayed, "God, I thank You for the Word. Now, I'll lay down for another hour or two and I'm trusting You to bless me physically, spiritually, emotionally today so that Your will is accomplished."

Later, I got up and went to work and because of severe weather, the service was canceled for that night (a rare occasion for service to be canceled) and I had another week to prepare! HALLELUJAH!

God was so faithful! During the week, I received another answer to a prayer request from the previous month. On Wednesday, November 4, I was informed about a social worker position with DaVita Dialysis Clinics in Hinesville/Baxley. I had applied for it and was transferred. I no longer had to alternate driving to Metter, Vidalia, and Wrightsville every week.

On my Dad's birthday, Friday, December 4, I did not have to travel to Wrightsville (over 2 hours one way). Because of his birthday celebration that weekend, I wanted that day off and since I had already put in my thirty-two hours, I was automatically off.

The Communion Service

The communion service took place on Wednesday, December 9, and some excerpts from my message are below:

> *In the recent past, I allowed my distress to affect my duty, obligation, and privilege of partaking in communion. All I could recall was hearing my uncle say as he read the scripture, 'He that eateth and drinketh unworthily eateth and drinketh damnation to himself, not discerning the Lord's body. For this cause many are weak and sickly among you, and many sleep.' I thought, SLEEP? I don't want that to happen to me. God dealt with me. If I live EVERY day, EVERY moment as if Jesus were about to return, then I would have no problem partaking in the Lord's Supper.*

> *There can be turmoil all around me, but that doesn't mean there has to be turmoil inside of me. So, if I look like a stranger, it's because I stayed away. But I thank God for His mercy. Communion isn't a meaningless ritual. It's one of the sacraments of our church. It's about remembering Christ's death and maintaining fellowship with Him. As long as I stay in communion with God, I will have no*

problem taking communion. So, I repented. I had already told God I would start coming back in January. Well, as you can see, God didn't intend for me to wait until then. I'm glad to be back. Thank you, Pastor and First Lady. (Bishop and First Lady Jackson were seated on the front row.)

No matter what you HAVE faced, what you're facing NOW, or what you WILL face, if you become broken, GOD WILL NOT THROW YOU AWAY.

If anyone knew about being broken, our Lord Jesus knew. None of what we go through can be compared with what He went through and what He endured for us.

Have you ever thrown away something that was broken and you thought it was useless? When you become broken, God DOES NOT throw you away, because He knows that He can still do something with you. He can still make something out of you.

Why is God turning the wheel and allowing things to happen and molding you and making you over? He wants to make you more in the image of His Son, Jesus Christ.

As the wheel turns, as situations come, as things happen, God intends for you to look more and more like Jesus. After God has made you over, He will make you whole.

If you started out broken, when God gets through with you, and makes you over, you will be at the opposite end of the spectrum. You can be made whole. The woman with the issue of blood put forth the effort to get closer to Jesus. When she touched the hem of His garment, she received her healing.

You have to want to be shaped and molded by God. It doesn't matter what YOUR ISSUE might be. You have to want to get closer to Jesus, to pray, to spend time in the Word, if you want to walk in victory and be more than a conqueror.

After you've been broken, made over, and made whole, you can be 'a vessel unto honor, sanctified, and meet for the master's use, and prepared unto every good work' (2 Timothy 2:21).

Before I take my seat, if you know Philippians 1:6, let's say it together and point to your

> *neighbor. If you don't have a neighbor, point to yourself...Are you ready?*
>
> **"Being confident of this very thing, that he which hath begun a good work in YOU will perform it until the day of Jesus Christ."**
>
> *If you've been Broken, you CAN be Made Over, you CAN be Made Whole, and you CAN be used by God. Amen.*

The message was so powerful, that not only were people in the congregation blessed that night, but years later and every now and then it still blesses, encourages, and helps me. I am so that that it does because every now and then we must encourage ourselves.

Me? Yes, You

You may be broken, but do not allow the enemy to tell you that you cannot be used by God. There may be guidelines and protocols for ministry that must be followed in your church and I understand that. Walk in obedience to your leadership. However, no one needs to have any special certifications, licenses or titles to obey the Great Commission found in Matthew 28:19-20.

Go therefore, and make disciples of all nations, baptizing them in the name of the Father, and of the Son, and of the Holy Spirit, teaching them to observe all things that I have commanded you; and lo, I am with you always, even to the end of the age. Amen. (NKJV)

When I read that word *disciple* in the passage above, I thought of how God gave Pastor Aaron (Bishop) and First Lady Christi Cowart the vision to start home discipleship groups (referred to as d-groups) for the first time the fall semester of 2019. It is based on Acts 2:42-47.

They devoted themselves to the apostles' teaching and to fellowship, to the breaking of bread and to prayer. Everyone was filled with awe, and many wonders and miraculous signs were performed by the apostles. All the believers were together and had everything in common...Every day they continued to meet together in the temple courts. They broke bread in their homes and ate together with glad and sincere hearts, praising God and enjoying the favor of all the people. And the Lord added to their number daily those who were being saved.

When I Was 40

The fall semester d-groups' list included various topics and books written by well-known authors. Some of the topics included "Boundaries" by Dr. Henry Cloud and Dr. John Townsend, "Financial Peace University" by Dave Ramsey, "Bait of Satan" by John Bevere, "Growing Through Divorce" by Jim Smoke, "The Five Love Languages" by Dr. Gary Chapman, and "Kingdom Single" by Dr. Tony Evans. I am honored that I was asked to lead a group.

Just before the end of December of 2018, I heard about "Kingdom Single" while listening to the radio. I knew it would not be available until July of 2019, and I felt very strongly that God was leading me to purchase it. Well, I was quite busy and sincerely forgot to get it. God had mercy on me and that was the d-group that I facilitated from August–November. Our God is so awesome! I was single again and He used me to disciple other singles.

Pastor Cowart announced that there were fifteen groups being held because over 200 people had signed up for the various topics. Because of the great response, a few topics were taught in more than one location. I am so grateful to be a part of Live Oak Church in Hinesville, Georgia. I am so glad that our leaders are teaching by example because they also facilitated a group in their home.

I believe that as we are making disciples, we are obeying the Great Commission.

Chapter 3

Me? Yes, You Reflections

Have you ever questioned whether God actually gave you an assignment?

_____

_____

When did you realize that He was, in fact, calling you to do it?

_____

_____

Have you ever hesitated to move forward out of fear or some other reason?

_____

_____

When I Was 40

Explain

_____

_____

Have you ever thought, "No, He can't be telling me to do that"?

_____

_____

Have you felt like God should use someone else and not use you?

_____

_____

How did you handle those feelings?

_____

_____

Do you still feel that way?

_____

_____

Whom have you discussed your feelings with?

_____

What are you going to do differently?

What are you personally doing to help fulfill the Great Commission in your area?

Take a few minutes to look up and reflect on the scriptures given in this chapter. Record what the Holy Spirit reveals to you from these scriptures as they relate to your life situation.

What does Jeremiah 1:8 say about being afraid of what others may think if you obey God?

How has this helped you move forward with God's call on your life?

When I Was 40

What did God say in Jeremiah 18:6 about the potter and the clay that ministered to you?

_____

_____

Romans 8:28-31 assures you that God has

_____

_____

2 Timothy 2:21 basically says no matter who you are, you are

_____

_____

Philippians 1:6 promises you

_____

_____

Matthew 28:19-20 says you are to

_____

_____

Me? Yes, You Reflections

Important Points and Notes from this Chapter

_____

_____

_____

_____

_____

_____

_____

_____

_____

_____

Pray: *Lord, thank You that You have called me to fulfill Your purpose in me. Please show me how You would have me fulfill the Great Commission of making disciples for Your kingdom.*

Chapter 4
A New Home **and** a New Job?

During this time, I was the leader of the Prayer Ministry at Mt. Zion Missionary Baptist Church in Hinesville, Georgia. We met at 6 a.m. on the first and third Saturdays. On March 6, 2010, I was able to walk for thirty minutes after our prayer service. I walked around the parking lot of the church. I also desired to eat breakfast with someone and Elder Joyce Scott (now First Lady Joyce Moore, Resurrection Christian Baptist Church in Jesup, Georgia) was available. We spent time together at Lowe's, then she treated me to a delicious meal at Waffle King. She also planted the thought of purchasing a home during our time together and told me about a house that was for sale in her neighborhood.

I was so grateful for how God was helping me. In the next nine days, He allowed me to recognize at least these areas where I was not exercising good stewardship:

When I Was 40

(1) overspending at Wal-Mart
(2) paying $566 for gas in 3 months (for cooking and heating at my single-wide trailer)
(3) paying rent instead of buying a home
(4) not consistently using a budget

I read 1 Peter 4:9 and continued to ask God to lead and direct me.

> *Be hospitable to one another without grumbling. As each one has received a gift, minister it to one another, as good stewards of the manifold grace of God.*

The next day, I reached out to another prayer partner, Elder Mabel Burford, who was also a realtor. I explained my situation and she was scheduled to show me a home right around $100,000, which was all I could afford at the time. She continued to do some research and told me that first-time homebuyers could get an $8,000 tax credit and second-time homebuyers could get a $6,000 tax credit. The contract had to be in progress by April 30 because the program expired on June 30, 2010.

I prayed, "God, if it's Your will for me to take advantage of that program then I ask You to work out all details. Find the place You want me to be, with all the space and storage and amenities I'll need for the price I can afford in Your timing. In Jesus' name!"

A New Home And A New Job?

At the same time I was discussing a new home, I was also looking for a new job. I enjoyed being a medical social worker, but I was ready to stop traveling to Baxley. Also, I really wanted a job on Ft. Stewart, Georgia. I had applied for two social worker jobs: a contract position and a direct-hire vacancy with the federal government. I'd passed my Licensed Master Social Worker exam in 2008, but I did not have enough clinical hours to sit for the LCSW nor did I have the substance abuse certification. However, they were willing to hire me with a probationary period to obtain the necessary credentials. The director over the contract position offered me a job first, but I waited. I did not decline or accept because I was focused on getting a federal job.

While talking to Ms. Mabel one day, I said, "Can God give me a new job and a new house at the same time?"

She said with excitement, "Yes, He can!"

She was such a great source of encouragement. I do not think I asked that question from a lack of faith. It was more of, "Wow, God, You're going to do this for me?"

He was about to blow my mind.

When I told my eleven-year-old son that I was praying for a job at Ft. Stewart, he said, "Mama, God gave you all the others."

I worked for the District Attorney's Office, Hinesville, Georgia from 1989-1999. I worked for the Department of Family and Children Services (Liberty and Long Counties) from 1999-2008. I worked for a local hospice and home care agency from May–November of 2008. I worked for DaVita Dialysis in Wrightsville, Metter, Vidalia and

When I Was 40

Savannah from December of 2008-December of 2009. I transferred to another region and covered clinics in Baxley and Hinesville from January - June of 2010. Finally, I was closer to home and it was wonderful.

Even my boy recognized God's favor on my life and that was very encouraging!

· 🖋 ·

After obtaining my LMSW in 2008, I started applying for federal jobs with the Veterans Administration. I had applied for quite a few positions over the last two-and-a-half years. Now, this job was not with the VA, but I finally had two interviews. (I was amazed how that was the perfect time for all of this to take place!)

Ms. Mabel agreed to walk with me through every step of the home building process. I could not have asked for a better realtor and prayer partner. My landlords at the time supported my decision to buy a home. The wife was a former realtor and was available to offer me advice. There would be no problem with getting out of the lease early because I had been a good tenant. All I had to do was give them two months' notice. Just a day or so later, Ms. Mabel called. She located a builder for me. I could build a new house for the price of buying the used one that we were planning to tour. I scheduled an appointment at my bank. Pre-approval was underway, and my loan officer forwarded my request to the mortgage department.

On Wednesday, I prayed for God to order my steps because I could not remember ever having to pray about a new house and a new job at the same time. I got the call for a new job offer and the call for my new home loan appointment on the same day. God is so awesome!

I asked for His perfect will to be done and for Him to be glorified in whatever happened.

· 🖋 ·

I went to Bible study that night and before going to bed, I prayed out loud, "Thank You, God, for all of the people praying for me. Thank You for my new job and my new home!"

On March 11, 2010, the lesson from Our Daily Bread was titled, "God's Mercies." The scripture reading was from Genesis 32:3-13 KJV. Verse ten says, "I am not worthy of the least of all the mercies, and of all the truth, which thou has shewed unto thy servant, for with my staff I passed over this Jordan; and now I am become two bands."

An excerpt from the lesson reads: *Humility and contrition are the keys that open the heart of God. As He did with Jacob, God hears us when we humbly cry out to Him for mercy. Mercy is an unearned blessing bestowed by God on an unworthy recipient.*

> *The sacrifices of God are a broken spirit, a broken and a contrite heart—These, O God, You will not despise.* (Psalm 51:17)

I told God, "I am not worthy. I'm not sitting on a huge bank account. I don't have all of the credentials they want for the job. But I have You. If You are for me, who can be against me. If You give me the house and job, I will give You the glory. Do it for Your glory. In Jesus' name."

It was such an exciting time! The builder that Ms. Mabel found was also a local resident. He had a certain floor plan already picked out for the small lot. I showed it to my Dad and he suggested that I ask if I could provide my own floor plan. I found one for about 1200 square feet, close to the same size as the one the builder had posted on the lot. Because of space, the only change we had to make was to swap the location of the master bedroom and bathroom with the kitchen and laundry room so that the side door would coincide with the driveway, which could not be moved. No problem. I enjoyed watching everything happen. Years prior to this, I really wanted to build a home, but I had never been able to do so.

It might have been a starter home, but it was an amazing experience for me and my son. Because I had not yet started my job on post, I was still traveling to and from Baxley, which was not too far, when compared to Wrightsville. Almost every day I drove by the house. If I were out of town, my Dad stopped by for me. My parents, siblings, loved ones, prayer partners, and friends were all so happy for me.

A New Home And A New Job?

During this time, my Mom spent some months in Texas with my sister, Denesia, and her sons, who were stationed at Ft. Bliss, so I kept her up to date on the building progress.

May 14, 2010 was the day we met at the attorney's office for the closing. I was able to use my lunch break to drive from the Hinesville clinic, sign the paperwork, and return to work with the keys to a brand-new house. I had to be out of my trailer by the end of May. I had a team of twelve close friends and prayer partners who helped me move out the last Saturday of the month.

I enjoyed finally living in the city limits. I had grown up in the country and always lived on the outskirts of town. This time, I lived in the house closest to the Ludowici–Long County Volunteer Fire Department. I was not expecting a fire or any type of emergency, but if I had one, all they had to do was just run over with the hose. I loved my cute little house and I started planning my housewarming. I built what I could afford. It was nice and cozy, and my son and I thoroughly enjoyed our time there.

Not only did I have help moving, but I also had loved ones and prayer partners who blessed me with furniture, appliances, interior decorations, gift cards, and monetary donations before, during, and after the housewarming. God supplied all of our needs. I sincerely appreciated every gift and every word of encouragement.

I worked for Liberty County for ten years and for the State of Georgia for seven years. My prayer had been to have a federal job by the age of forty. Well, I was interviewed and accepted the position while I was forty, but my first day of work was on Monday, June 21, 2010, just two days after I turned forty-one. My housewarming was on Saturday, June 26, 2010.

My God is awesome! He gave me a new job and a new home and I am still giving Him the glory!

· ∅ ·

While writing this, I have to say that my parents are extremely proud of not just me but all of my siblings as well. Over a year and a half ago, my brother resigned from his job at a college in Savannah, Georgia to pursue his dream of truck driving. He has his own truck now and he loves it. Denesia is proudly serving in the United States Army and her husband is now retired. Kimberly has been working with a local bank for several years and loves her job. All of my parents' grandchildren are either in school or are working and are doing very well.

Chapter 4
A New Home **and** a New Job? Reflections

When was the last time God answered several prayer requests for you all at the same time and you became overjoyed and almost overwhelmed?

_____

_____

Explain:

_____

_____

When I Was 40

If that has never happened to you, do you feel disappointed or angry with God?

_____

_____

Have you discussed those feelings with anyone?

_____

_____

Did you ever feel as if you didn't deserve God's blessings?

_____

_____

Have you come to realize that none of us actually deserve His blessings?

_____

_____

Do you understand that how we respond to God's blessings can bring much glory to Him?

_____

_____

A New Home And A New Job? Reflections

How are you handling the blessings God has already given you?
What do you need to do differently?

_____

_____

Take a few minutes to look up and reflect on the scriptures given in this chapter. Record what the Holy Spirit reveals to you from these scriptures as they relate to your life situation.

Psalm 51:17 says God looks for

_____

_____

What does 1 Peter 4:10 tell you about being a good steward of the gifts God has blessed you with?

_____

_____

Who has God used to bring you some of these blessings?

_____

_____

How have you shown appreciation to them and to God for all these gifts and blessings?

_____

_____

Are there those you need to express your appreciation to?

_____

_____

Remember to give God all the glory for the wonderful ways He has blessed you.

> *For everyone to whom much is given, from him much will be required; and to whom much has been committed, of him they will ask the more.* (Luke 12:48)

Important Points and Notes from this Chapter

_____

_____

_____

_____

_____

_____

_____

_____

_____

Pray: *Thank You, Heavenly Father, for the many gifts and blessings You have given me. I thank You for those You have used to bless me. Please bless them for their generosity to me. I give You all the praise and glory for the great things You have done and are doing in my life. In Jesus' name I pray. Amen.*

Chapter 5
Steps Ordered

In the Introduction, I stated I have attended church for as long as I could remember. The timeline below shows every church where I was a member or regular attendee.

I attended Junior Church of Christ, Holiness Unto the Lord (now Kingdom Church of Christ) in Riceboro, Georgia, Bishop E.L. Stevens, from childhood until I married Paul Williams in December of 1988.

From December of 1988 until we felt God leading us to move on in July of 1998, we attended St. John Church of Christ, Holiness Unto the Lord in Ludowici, Georgia, Elder Howard McArthur, then later Elder David Nelson, Sr. under the direction of Bishop Moses Lewis.

From July-September of 1998, we attended Mt. Zion Missionary Baptist Church in Hinesville, Georgia, Pastor (now Bishop) M.L. Jackson. We joined in October of that year. I remained a member of Mt. Zion for 12 years until I felt God leading me to move on in July of 2010.

When I Was 40

From August of 2010 until I married Benjamin Jenkins in February of 2013, I attended River of Life Ministries in Allenhurst, Georgia under Bishop Leotha and Apostle Curley Walthour.

Ben and I were not members, but we attended Compass Worship Center in Ludowici, Georgia, Pastor David Holton, from February of 2013-February of 2014.

From March–September of 2014, we attended Live Oak Church of God in Hinesville, Georgia. (Pastors are Bishop Israel Aaron and First Lady Christi Cowart.). We joined and became covenant partners in October of 2014. Ben ended up in the hospital before the end of that month. He had open-heart surgery in November, and sadly he passed away in December. I have remained at LOC. I told a few people that Ben dropped me off here on his way to heaven.

This is where God has planted me and allowed me to start Celebrate Recovery, a Christ-centered recovery program that helps people gain freedom from their hurts, habits, and hang-ups. CR is in over 35,000 churches in the world. If I had never experienced any hardship, I would not have been able to help others through theirs.

God Ordered My Steps

Now that you have a snapshot of my starting and ending points, I need to go back and focus on some details that are just confirmation of how God has been ordering my steps.

My family and I began attending Mt. Zion Missionary Baptist Church in July of 1998 (the month before our son was born). During our years as members, we operated in various capacities including deacon, deaconess, maintenance, media, minister, prayer ministry, and puppet ministry.

I filed for divorce in July of 2009 and it was final in September. I continued to operate in my role as Ministry of Arts Coordinator until December of 2009. I felt God leading me to resign, and my assistant, Elder Janice Hill, became the new leader. I continued to lead the Prayer Ministry until May of 2010. When God led me to resign, my assistant, Elder Tia Garrett, became the new leader.

She asked, "Charlene, where are you going? You've resigned from leading the Ministry of Arts and now from leading the Prayer Ministry."

I replied, "I don't know where I'm going, but I'm obeying God."

> *Trust in the LORD with all your heart,*
>
> *and lean not on your own understanding;*
>
> *In all your ways acknowledge Him, And He shall direct your paths.* (Proverbs 3:5-6)

Then on the first Sunday in June of 2010, I was visiting River of Life Ministries. My uncle, Leotha Walthour, Sr. (now deceased) was being installed as Bishop. I had attended the 8 a.m. service at Mt. Zion so I could attend this special installation service with my family. While I was there that day, I heard God tell me that I needed to be a part of that ministry. I was so confident and at peace about it, before the end of the day, I informed my current and future pastors of my decision.

I went home and avoided praying about the departure date for about a week. I just didn't want to know yet. Finally, I had to ask God when and He gave me the date. The fourth Sunday in July was my last one at Mt. Zion. I attended Bible Study that Wednesday, and I knew I would be at River of Life on the first Sunday in the following month, which was August 1, 2010.

Early that morning, while in prayer, I asked God why I had to start attending the new church on THAT day and He said, "New beginning" (1st day of the 8th month). God gave me the instructions while I was still forty, but by the time I started attending, I was already forty-one.

> ***Every church I have attended, I knew God had me there for a specific reason and appointed season.***

• 🖋 •

I want to say thank you to every pastor and every leader that has helped to shape me into the person I am today. As I reflect on the list above, I am amazed at how I was able to remember the exact months and years that I attended each church. I can say with certainty that I never left any of them because I just got tired of being there or because people got on my nerves. I always waited until I felt God leading me to do so. Much prayer went into the decision and departure did not happen without the peace of God.

My steps are still being ordered and you can read more about how in my next book.

> *The steps of a good man are ordered by the LORD, and He delights in his way. Though he fall, he shall not be utterly cast down; For the LORD upholds him with His hand.* (Psalm 37:23-24)

Chapter 5
Steps Ordered Reflections

Have you ever felt like God was instructing you to leave a place where you were comfortable and relocate to a different place?

_____

_____

How did you feel about that?

_____

_____

Were you immediately obedient? If so, what happened next?

_____

_____

If you were not obedient right away, what happened next?

___

___

Did you ever discuss this decision with anyone?

___

___

Have you learned that obeying God is important in order to grow spiritually?

___

___

Explain:

___

___

Is there anything that you need to do differently in the future?

___

___

Steps Ordered Reflections

Explain:

_____

_____

Take a few minutes to look up and reflect on the scriptures given in this chapter. Record what the Holy Spirit reveals to you from these scriptures as they relate to your life situation.

Proverbs 3:5-6 says if we,

_____

_____

then God will.

_____

_____

What are the promises given to you in Psalm 37:23-24?

1. _____

2. _____

3. _____

4. _____

When I Was 40

How have these promises changed the way you pray and make decisions?

_____

_____

Important Points and Notes from this Chapter

_____

_____

_____

_____

_____

_____

_____

_____

Pray: *Thank You, Father God, that my steps are ordered by You. Thank You, that though I may face challenges in my life, I* *shall not be utterly cast down for I know You uphold me with Your hand. Remind me to always seek Your direction before I make a life decision knowing Your way is always the right way. In Jesus' name I pray. Amen.*

Chapter 6
Visible Difference

While completing this final chapter, I could not help but compare my two pictures in the back of this book. I look years younger now than I did when I was forty! People sometimes guess that I am still in my thirties or forties. I have been told, "You don't look like what you've been through!" I definitely thank God for that! It is obvious from the photos that I am at least twenty pounds lighter now. My peaceful state is evident on my countenance. I am healthier and I am so grateful for the changes I have been making in my daily life.

One change I have made is that I am not weighed down spiritually. Why? Because I have learned to stop carrying burdens. Also, I have stopped pretending to be something that I am not. I am not wearing any more masks. I love our motto at Live Oak Church: *Real People, Real Issues, Real God.*

It is so liberating to know that God can still use me even though I have made mistakes along the way.

· 𝒪 ·

My desire is to always be available for God to use me, so I am taking better care of myself. I sincerely enjoy being in His presence. Spending time with God by reading my Bible and making time for prayer are a priority for me every day. Even if I am in a hurry because I overslept, I can still read and meditate on one verse. I can still say breath prayers. I have scriptures as reminders on my cell phone. I would rather meditate on the Word than to dwell on negativity. I do not hold grudges and I try to repent and make amends as soon as possible. Being quick to repent has helped me to overcome selfishness.

Taking care of myself also includes walking, which I enjoy. I take advantage of opportunities to walk from my office to the cafeteria several times a week. I have been known to walk a bit fast in the building. I have to get my heart rate up! I have not caused any collisions, but I must admit that I have been asked to slow down in the sanctuary. I am so accustomed to walking fast everywhere I go that I just do not realize when I am walking too fast for the indoors. I enjoy walking so much that when I go to Wal-Mart, most of the time, I park my car closer to Wendy's than I do to the actual store.

In addition to exercise, I have tried to drink eight cups of water daily. I may even get up to a gallon, but only on the weekend, for obvious reasons. Some months ago, my son and I were at the dinner table. That has been a favorite place for me to just fellowship with my children and family. As we ate that day, he challenged me to eat some jalapenos with him and I abruptly declined.

He playfully said, "You wimp."

Right away, I invited him to drink a gallon of water with me and he also declined my invitation.

Then I said, "You wimp."

We laughed. At least we both knew our limits. I drink mostly water, green tea, fruit juice, unsweetened almond milk, and lemonade. Occasionally, I'll have sweet or flavored tea, coffee, and ginger ale (for an upset stomach). I stopped consuming soft drinks back in the fall of 2011 and I do not miss them.

Along with changes in what I drink, I have also changed my food choices. I try to eat more fruits, vegetables, nuts, and whole grains. I limit sugar and sweets. If I eat meat, it is usually chicken, fish, or turkey. I have gotten away from eating some of the meats that I grew up eating.

When I was growing up, Daddy was a hunter, and Mama has always been a great cook. You should try her biscuits. She can cook much more than that, but I think people request her biscuits more than they request anything else. I loved to eat whatever she fixed. My brother, on the other hand, would eat white rice with milk if he did not want what was prepared. I have no idea how his substitute tasted, because I don't think I had ever tried it or maybe I tried it once and did not like it. I preferred the rice and gravy and whatever meat and vegetables Mama had prepared.

To this day, my brother says, "I don't eat organs."

I can't blame him. Although I still love to eat, I have chosen to remove the organs from my diet as well! I have discovered in my research that with my mouth, I can speak life, but at the same time eat myself to death! The older I get, the more I am learning how to use food as a medicine to promote better health.

By the way, I did not mention my sisters above because they were not born yet. While my brother and I were growing up, we asked for more siblings as additional playmates. Daddy and Mama did eventually grant our request (we knew it had nothing to do with us). I was seventeen when Denesia was born and nineteen when Kimberly was born. My brother and I grew up together and our younger sisters grew up together. I don't remember much about their eating habits. I was out of the house when Daddy and Mama brought Kim home from the hospital. All I know is that those two do not like bananas because Mama did not like bananas.

Better health also means better mental health. I am a licensed clinical social worker and I am trying to practice what I recommend to my patients. One thing I teach is living in a state of mindfulness. I try to stay in the here and now. It's been ten years since I have taken medication for depression and anxiety. I have noticed that if I am feeling depressed, it's because of something that happened that I cannot undo. If I am feeling anxious, it's because of something that has not yet happened. The Serenity Prayer sits on my desk and I use it for myself, too. I try my best to control my emotions and not let my emotions control me.

Serenity Prayer
Written by Reinhold Neibuhr (1892-1971)

God grant me the serenity
To accept the things I cannot change;
Courage to change the things I can;
And wisdom to know the difference.
Living one day at a time;
Enjoying one moment at a time;
Accepting hardships as the pathway to peace;
Taking, as He did, this sinful world
As it is, not as I would have it;
Trusting that He will make all things right
If I surrender to His Will;
So that I may be reasonably happy in this life
And supremely happy with Him
Forever and ever in the next.
Amen.[4]

I have found that serenity and peace have nothing to do with my circumstances. I can be surrounded by turmoil but still be at peace in my mind. I can do that because my strength comes from God and because I am an optimist. I

---

[4] https://www.thevoiceforlove.com/serenity-prayer.html

have learned that it is impossible to think negatively and end up with a positive life. Whatever I think about is what I will bring about.

"For as he thinketh in his heart, so is he." (Proverbs 23:7 KJV)

· 🖋 ·

Because I am more mindful of taking care of myself, I am more mindful of how I treat others. I speak life, not just to myself, but also to others. I try to be an encourager. Because I try to encourage others, I am also encouraged *by* others. 2 Corinthians 1:3-5 says because God has comforted us in all our tribulations, we are to comfort and encourage others.

I am never lonely. I try to maintain contact with my children, parents, siblings, and loved ones. I also have at least three levels of friends: mentors, mentees, and peers. I make sure that I have access to people and prayer partners if I'm having a rough moment. I am available to pour into others while also being poured into by others. I have my church family, Pastors, fellow laborers, and the Spiritual Life Team. I also have my superiors, peers, coworkers, and colleagues. I have my Celebrate Recovery Family and my newest group of Kingdom Single Disciples.

Several months ago, a coworker told me that I never act like I'm having a bad day. I told him it's because I spend time with God before coming into the office. I must be in the right frame of mind so that I can be all there for my patients and coworkers.

God helps me to overcome any difficulties I may encounter each day.

I love to smile and laugh, and I enjoy making others laugh. I love music. (I prefer writing over singing.) In fact, I have released two singles: a Christmas song entitled *Jesus Christ is Coming Again* and *Be Nice, Save A Life,* an anti-bullying song. Both are available for digital download at amazon.com.

As you can see, I am taking care of myself spiritually, physically, mentally, and emotionally. I am doing my best to take care of this temple because it's the only one I get here on earth. I know that God has placed me here for His glory and to bring Him pleasure and not to do what pleases myself. All that I do daily involves making Him happy and making Him proud. If my entire focus is to please God, I cannot help but be full of joy!

Galatians 6:8-10 says, "For he who sows to his flesh will of the flesh reap corruption, but he who sows to the Spirit will of the Spirit reap everlasting life. And let us not grow weary while doing good, for in due season we shall reap if we do not lose heart. Therefore, as we have opportunity, let us do good to all, especially to those who are of the household of faith."

When I Was 40

In closing, it is great when there are noticeable differences in my physique. What's even better is when people can see the differences in my character. I can look in the mirror and make changes when I am not pleased with what I see. Well, the Word of God is just like a mirror. It reflects what is in my heart. When my time with God reveals my character defects, I ask for His help, strength, grace, and forgiveness. Then, I make the necessary adjustments. As I grow older, I don't want to be stubborn and set in my ways. I want people to see more of Jesus and less of Charlene.

Chapter 6
Visible Difference Reflections

When was the last time you looked at pictures of yourself from years ago and made comparisons?

_____

_____

Are you pleased with the changes you have made?

_____

_____

Explain:

_____

_____

When I Was 40

Do you wish you looked the way you did then or are you pleased with your current appearance?

_____

_____

Explain:

_____

_____

What are you doing to make necessary changes?

_____

_____

What about the part of you that no one can see? Who are you when no one is watching you?

_____

_____

Are you happy with the person you have become, or do you want to make some changes?

_____

_____

Visible Difference Reflections

Explain:

_____

_____

When was the last time you spent time in the Word of God and desired to change?

_____

_____

If you have breath, you have another chance because God's mercies are new every morning. What's keeping you from making the necessary changes?

_____

_____

When are you going to do something about it?

_____

_____

Take a few minutes to look up and reflect on the scriptures given in this chapter. Record what the Holy Spirit reveals to you from these scriptures as they relate to your life situation.

When I Was 40

What does Proverbs 23:7a say about what we focus our thoughts on?

_____

_____

Do you need to make some changes in your thinking?

_____

_____

How can you make these changes?

_____

_____

2 Corinthians 1:3-5 says we are to:

_____

_____

What are you doing to obey what this says you should be doing?

_____

_____

Visible Difference Reflections

What instructions did you receive from Galatians 6:8-10?

1. Do not

_____

_____

2. Do

_____

_____

3. Do not

_____

_____

4. Do

_____

_____

5. Do

_____

_____

When I Was 40

Are you following these instructions?

_____

_____

Are there some things you need to do differently?

_____

_____

Explain:

_____

_____

Important Points and Notes from this Chapter

_____

_____

_____

_____

_____

_____

_____

_____

_____

Pray: *Father God, please show me areas where I am not reflecting Your heart and compassion for those around me. Help me to be more sensitive to the promptings of Your Holy Spirit so that I am an encourager not only with my words but with my actions as well. Thank You for using me to reflect Your glory. In Jesus' name I pray. Amen.*

Epilogue

I did it! This project has been on my heart for almost ten years. I mentioned it to a few loved ones. They all were very supportive because they knew my story. Even though I wish I had not waited so long to complete it, I sincerely believe it was finished at the right time. On Thursday, November 8, 2018, I was sitting at my desk at the end of the lunch period when I felt God was leading me to get started on this book. It had to be God, because I would not have decided to do this on my own. I am busy enough. I have a full-time job. I am the Ministry Leader of Celebrate Recovery at Live Oak Church, which includes the Large Group on Mondays and a step study with a smaller group of women on another night of the week. I also have other ministry-related duties and I enjoy them all.

I may have an empty nest, but I still have three adult children plus my parents and siblings. I did not want to isolate myself too much in the process. It felt so good to start typing my manuscript on Saturday, November 10 (Aaron's birthday). I said earlier that I had mentioned this to a few people. Well, there is one person I did not have to mention it to, because somehow, he knew.

Just before the end of 2018, I heard from my close friend and prayer partner, Daric Dearman. We had not talked on the phone or seen each other in over two years. However, we continued to communicate via text every few months or so.

During that first conversation, he asked, "Have you written your book?"

I never told him about writing a book. I had inquired about *his*, which I'm looking forward to reading one day.

"You're going to write a lot of books," he said. "How could you not write a book with all you've been through? You're a thinker. God's going to use you."

I finally admitted that I was obedient and had started writing the previous month. That discussion was just another confirmation that it was time. Remembering and reflecting on what God did during that short period of my life only helped me to recognize His divine providence.

I certainly hope that your reflections will give insight and revelation about what God has done and what He will do *for* you and *through* you. I am very thrilled I'm able to finally share this part of my story with you. I know God still has great things in store for me.

You might be wondering what happened from age forty-one until now, so I will share this little bit with you. I was diagnosed with breast cancer at the age of forty-four, just a few months after marrying Benjamin. In January of 2014, I went through breast cancer surgery, followed by six

Epilogue

weeks of radiation. Then, I made it through Ben's death in December of that year. We were still newlyweds when he passed away. You can read all about how God helped me to be a "SURVIVOR" in my second book, which will be released in the coming months.

For updates on its availability, you may visit my website at: www.charlenestevensjenkins.com

Tom Tripplett Park, Pooler, Georgia. We had such a great time on the morning of April 3, 2020 that I just had to share some of those moments.

Nicole Newton, Perfect Portraits

When I Was 40

Epilogue

When I Was 40

More Reflections

You are our epistle written in our hearts, known and read by all men; clearly you are an epistle of Christ, ministered by us, written not with ink but by the Spirit of the living God, not on tablets of stone but on tablets of flesh, that is, of the heart. (2 Corinthians 3:2-3)

What did Paul mean when he said those who had witnessed his ministry were epistles to be read by all men?

_____

_____

Have you ever thought of writing a book?

_____

_____

When I Was 40

Has anyone ever told you that you should write a book?

_____

_____

Why?

_____

_____

What will it be about?

_____

_____

Have you shared your ideas with anyone?

_____

_____

Why or why not?

_____

_____

Have you started on it?

_____

_____

More Reflections

If not, what's keeping you from getting started?

_____

_____

Did you know that someone is waiting to read **your** story?

_____

_____

What are you believing God for that others think is impossible to accomplish?

_____

_____

Do **you** think that it can be done?

_____

_____

Why or why not?

_____

_____

What does Philippians 4:13 tell you?

_____

_____

What have you learned about, decided upon, or discovered from reading this book?

_____

_____

What are you going to do differently starting today?

_____

_____

Pray: *Father God, thank You that I can do all things through Christ who strengthens me. Show me what You want me to do with all that I learned from this book. In Jesus' name I pray. Amen.*

Final Word of Encouragement from Charlene...

As you go through life, you will experience accomplishments, challenges, and life lessons, some of which you may not wish to face again! While you are alive, you will encounter hardship and pain to some degree. The important thing is to make sure that you learn something from those experiences and move forward. If you want to discover how Charlene endured her challenges, then read this book. She relied on her faith and loved ones for support. Not only will you be reading about her life, but you will also be reflecting and answering your own questions. Hopefully, what you learn about yourself will enable you to make important decisions about your future choices. Then, somewhere down the road, you may be writing your own book! Why not? You have a story that needs to be shared and one that is worth reading about.

On my 50th Birthday. Photo taken by Nicole Newton, owner and operator of Perfect Portraits, Hinesville, Georgia.

My Mother, Jean Stevens and my son, Paul Williams, Jr. are helping to celebrate my 40th Birthday at Pelican Point, Crescent, Georgia.

About the Author

Charlene Stevens Jenkins stands at just about five feet in stature, but her impact on the lives of others is unforgettable. She is a Licensed Clinical Social Worker serving active duty soldiers assigned to the Ft. Stewart Army Installation in Southeast Georgia. It is her dream job and each day brings a fresh opportunity. For more than ten years she has helped people as a licensed clinical social worker and four years has volunteered as the Celebrate Recovery Ministry Leader at Live Oak Church of God, Hinesville, Georgia. Before joining Live Oak years ago, Charlene suffered quietly in a twenty-year marriage. The marriage ended in divorce, and Charlene began a journey of self-discovery and insight. Other tragedies hit her life, but faith in God and encouragement from friends and family -- including her three adult children are paramount to her story today.